G000060177

THE
NATURAL HISTORY
OF THE
BALLET GIRL

DANCE BOOKS
CECIL COURT LONDON

This edition published 1996 by
Dance Books Ltd
15 Cecil Court, London WC2N 4EZ.

ISBN 1 85273 046 3

Printed and bound in Great Britain by
Biddles Ltd, Guildford, Surrey.

THE NATURAL HISTORY

OF THE

BALLET-GIRL

BY ALBERT SMITH.

ILLUSTRATED BY A. HENNING.

LONDON: D. BOGUE, 86 FLEET STREET.

MDCCCXLVII.

The Ballet-master is now all excitement. Every time he bangs the tambourine, it is a signal for them to turn, or divide, simultaneously; and they wait for the same signal at night.

PREFACE.

SHOULD any Gent imagine, from the title of this little book, that he is "going to be put up to a thing or two," or, that there is anything in it which might, with propriety, exclude it from the drawing-room table — added to the commonly-circulated notions of the class we are about to write of — then is that Gent mistaken. We know what are his notions of the ballet generally—we are perfectly aware that he considers it "fast" to have the "Pets," coloured and framed, hung up in his rooms, to induce a belief in the breast of the visitor that he is on very intimate terms with the originals. We know, too, that he imagines, when in the front of the pit, he has but to wink at a fairy to be immediately received as her accepted admirer; and that, in fact, every female connected with the theatrical profession, without an exception, comes in the same category. But for the Gents we are not now writing. We never are, indeed, except for the purpose of insulting them and putting them in a rage with us. And so the Gent, who anticipates "something spicy" from the title of this *brochure*, had better put it down and regret his shilling quietly, before he flings it away in disgust.

For we intend to touch but lightly upon

pink-tights and gauze-petticoats. Spangles will only be hinted at; and wreaths almost passed by. We shall knock over theatrical romance for common-place reality; and try if we cannot make the one as interesting as the other, even by reversing the ordinary effect of glamour, and bringing down the innumerable muslin-petticoats — excelling even the capes of a night cabman's coat in the number of their layers — to the ordinary gown of everyday life.

After the unceasing labours of Cuvier, Linnæus, Buffon, Shaw, and other animal-fanciers on a large scale, had surmounted the apparently impossible task of marshalling all the earth's living curiosities into literary rank and file, a worthy old clergyman, at some little out-of-the-way village in Hampshire, put together his observations of several years in the Natural History of Selbourne; and its sparrows, grubs, and tortoises. And so we follow with this our Social Zoology, after more elaborate essays on different varieties of the human race.   We have disposed of The Vermin in the Gents.   Let us hope in the Ballet-girl we may now take up a more agreeable subject — The Butterflies.

THE NATURAL HISTORY

OF

THE BALLET-GIRL.

CHAPTER I.

OF FAIRIES AND BALLET-GIRLS.

ONCE upon a time — that dearly - loved old epoch in which we all so steadfastly believe, vague and unsatisfactory as is its real date — that golden age when the world was a series of summer forest glades, palaces, and kingdoms; peopled only by kings, ogres, virtuous woodcutters, enchanted princes, white cats, and beautiful daughters—there were Fairies in our land.

And there was also a month of May; but not like the one just over. Oh! no;—it was the May of England in the olden time— such a fair season as awakened the numbers of our early poets, and produced those bland and honest verses in honour of the "sote monthe," with which, in the joyousness of their hearts, they welcomed in the coming of Spring's fairest handmaiden. Nor was this homely feeling of rural glee confined to the poets alone, for all the land partook of it. And when they saw the blossoms and buds bursting from their winter shelter, and breaking forth into life and vitality, their own unaffected hearts inspired the feeling from the wild flowers, and they felt the influence of May, and rejoiced at her coming, with the same outpouring of breathing gratitude and homage that the flowers evinced by their sweet odours.

These were pleasant times, and the presence of the Fairies must have immensely increased the enjoyment. We wish they would come back again. They tell us Fairies are still in Ireland, but we do not believe it. If they were there, and did but a tenth part of the good to starving cottagers which their predecessors were in the habit of effecting, the place of " our own commissioner" would become a sinecure.

A favourite pursuit of these little people was, that of relieving the surplus cottage population by carrying off some child of earth with golden hair to live with them. Sometimes, to be sure, they merely made an interchange of infants, and left some remarkable brat in place of the proper one, who always behaved in the most unseemly manner, playing such pranks as we can only associate with Mr. Wieland when he was a baby. But more frequently they simply kept their mortal plaything until it was old enough to return to its parents, with a piece of ¹airy gold hung about its neck.

There is a delightful little German story of a child who was thus carried off, to whom the Fairies showed all their sports. "One while they danced by moonlight," says the chronicler, "on the primrose banks: at another time they skipped from bough to bough among the trees that hung over the cooling streams; for they moved as lightly and easily through the air as on the ground; and Mary went with them everywhere, for they bore her in their arms wherever they wished to go. Sometimes they would throw seeds on the turf, and directly little trees sprung up; and then they would set their feet upon the branches while the trees grew under them, till they danced upon the boughs in the air wherever the breezes carried them; and again the trees would sink down into the earth, and land them safely at their bidding. At other times they would go and visit the palace of their queen; and there the richest food was spread before them, and the softest music was heard: and there all around grew flowers which were always changing their hues from scarlet to purple, and yellow, and emerald. Sometimes they went to look at the heaps of treasure which were piled up in the royal stores: for little dwarfs were always employed in searching the earth for gold."

This must have been a pleasant life. Clever literary gentlemen will call it all nonsense, and say we are quoting trash. If none of us ever commit ourselves to a greater extent than in placing a little mild idle belief in the fairies, and loving to talk about them, we shall not become very bad, albeit we may run the risk of not writing "with a purpose." But books written with a purpose, beyond that of amusing, are sometimes so slow! And when the purpose is now and then so hazy as to almost be altogether invisible, but little is gained thereby.

We are forgetting the Ballet-girl though, all this time. Her early life must be some-

thing like that of the fairy changeling, and this
led us to speak of it.   We must except, however, the piece of gold hung round the neck.
This is most probably imitated by a bit of hol-
lowed out pewter, polished in various concavi-
ties, and called, in the terms of theatrical jew-
elry, a *Logie*.   Elsewise she is accustomed to
see phenomena quite as remarkable as any that
the elfs ever showed to the little girl in the
story.   But of this anon.

A LOGIE.

CHAPTER II.

OSSIBLY it has never been your good (or ill) fortune to be much behind the scenes at a theatre. Because if you have, and ventured to a morning rehearsal—of which we shall anon speak—it is not unlikely, should you blunder through the darkness into the green-room, you will there

find a small pale child undergoing a lesson
from the Ballet-mistress before the others arrive.   She looks as if she had been generated
from the atmosphere of a play-house, as spon-
taneously as were the galvanic mites of Mr.
Crosse, apparently from nothing.

She has on a curious dress—ballet from the waist downwards; ordinary walking costume above that point. Indeed, her appearance will remind you of the old woman in the nursery tale, who fell asleep on the highway, instead of selling her eggs at market; and whose petticoats were cut all about her knees by one Stout, an inhuman pedlar, so that even her little dog did not know her.

This is the Ballet-girl in her first stage of transition from the flying fairy—the stages being Fairy, Extra, Corps de Ballet, and Coryphée. Hitherto, she has only been slung to a wire, and moved across the stage, with a wreath of glazed calico flowers in her hand to herald in a benignant genius, or guide a rightful prince to his love. Or perhaps she has been perched upon an aerial machine to wave a silver yardmeasure with a star on the top; but now she is for the first time allowed to touch the earth before an audience. Her pay is at present very little—very little indeed—perhaps a shilling a night: and for this she has to trot backwards and forwards upon her thin legs, between her home and the theatre, sometimes four times a day; and it is possible she may live at Islington or Kennington.   Perhaps her father is a supernumerary, and he accompanies her; or she is confided to the care of an older sister Coryphée; or she makes the journey by herself.

This goes on for two or three years, and she is then, possibly, regularly apprenticed to a Ballet-master. Her life is here not altogether passed in attitudes, or on the points of her toes. She may be called upon to execute the domestic *pas* of fetching the beer, or even peeling the potatoes, for the Terpsichorean dinner: and her leisure time, when she gets any, which is but seldom, is passed in sitting with her feet in a peculiarly agonizing pair of stocks, which induce the power of pointing the toes until they form a line with the leg. At last, she finds herself pronounced competent to dance with others ; and gradually working her way from the rear ranks to the second, or if not that, immediately behind it, she has fifteen shillings a-week—a perfect fortune.

If you again saw this child with similar little people at night, they would probably be asleep amongst some of the machinery, having been tied to a floating cloud in the first scene, or danced after a car, and then dismissed, as not wanted, until the conclusion. Their night's work only commences when the night is far advanced ; and the effects of this artificial existence are usually painfully visible. Their lips are parched and fevered ; their cheeks hollow and pale, even in spite of the daub of vermillion hastily applied by the dresser ; and their limbs nipped and wasted. To the audience, however, they are smiling elves, who appropriately people the " Realms of Joy," to the centre of which blissful region their presence is confined.

Contrast them with the other children amongst the audience, to whose amusement these little creatures minister. *They* are not asleep, nor are they even tired—not they : for every means that could be devised to lessen the fatigue attendant upon this one instance of prolonged " going to bed " has been carefully put into practice. You cannot help comparing their real elfin mirth with the forced smiles of the little fictitious spirits we have just alluded to. And most beautiful to all—although all cannot tell at the moment from what agency their own sudden exhilaration springs—is their sunny and unalloyed laughter, which rings in joyous peals from one box to another, clear and musical above the coarser shouts of merriment that greet any unforeseen comicality.

For there are few more pleasant things in life, in this matter-of-fact, conventional world of ours, than taking a child for the first time to a play : there is nothing that re-opens the springs of

old feelings and recollections with such a burst
of gladness, however closed up and encrusted
over the well may be, by rust accumulated from
the damp of disappointment and the chill of
worldly buffeting and unrealized hope. Their
mirth is truly glorious: glorious from its purity
and reality; glorious from its inspiring effects
upon our own nipped and tarnished spirits. And
Heaven forbid that there should be any whose
withered sympathies are not refreshed by it:
for they must either be proof against all pleasant emotions, or never have known what a
home was when they numbered no more years
than the joyous children around them.

CHAPTER III.

OF THE MORNING REHEARSAL.

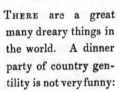

THERE are a great many dreary things in the world. A dinner party of country gentility is not very funny: neither can be a wet Sunday in a steady family at Clapham; or a sojourn at Worthing in bad weather. Anything pertaining to High Art is safe not to amuse you much: the Ancient

Concerts must be terribly slow affairs (but we were never there, preferring Jullien); and we don't believe much in the liveliness of " fine old standard comedies," having that degraded taste which would always lead us rather to pay our money to see Carlotta Grisi in Giselle, than anybody in the *School of Reform*. Vauxhall Gardens in the middle of January is not an exciting place: nor is Exeter Hall in the middle of May. Railway stations, when you have to wait there for an hour, are depressing at any time: and we mistrust "At Homes" given to collect wonderful people together.

But if you never had the opportunity of seeing a theatre by day-light and in the morning, you do not know to what extent dreariness can go. Let us accompany the Ballet-girl throughout her theatrical day.

It is eleven o'clock in the morning, and the rehearsal of a spectacle is about to take place. We fix upon this species of entertainment as it

offers more varied phases for description than a
simple Ballet.   It is a spectacle, then; with a
divertissement introduced; and perhaps an army
of Female Warriors.   At the stage door there
is a " call" wafered up: a little piece of paper
on which is a summons written in a cramped,
but clear hand, which you read thus :—

Wednesday, June 2

Ladies of the Ballet . . at 10.

All the Ladies and Gents :

Full Band . . . . . . at 11.

We pass a few of those anomalous untidy
people, who are always found waiting for something or somebody at stage doors—friends of the
first citizens, connections of the thunder, and
hangers-on of the establishment for the chance

of an engagement to do anything.   Just within is another class of loiterers, whom the stage-
door-keeper allows to stand there.   It is equally
difficult to tell what class they belong to, or
what they want.   They have all a dirty, almost
mouldy, appearance ; and are seldom seen anywhere else, except in the upper tiers of the
boxes, when the admission cards are not sus-
pended.   Passing them we reach the stage,
blinking and blinded from coming out of the
light.   The view is not exhilarating when you
can see.   All the scenes and sides—the " flats"
and " wings" as they are technically called—are
drawn away.   And above, some dirty day-
light is struggling through a wonderful confusion of ropes, borders, pulleys, and frail bridges ;
and some equally dingy rays pour in over the
back of the gallery.   All the fronts of the
boxes are still covered by the large canvas
cloths, which you always find the men so anxious to let down before the audience have left

the house, as though a great wager depended
upon their success in this respect. Two or
three brooms appear in the obscurity to be
knocking about by themselves amongst the
dark benches of the pit; and the faint glim-
mer of a candle is now and then seen flitting
along the lobbies, through the little holes in the
back of the box doors, or in the extreme depths
of the private boxes.

Perhaps at the back of the stage some of
the carpenters are nailing the water to a cas-
cade, or "priming" a scene with whitewash.
At a rickety table, in a front corner, is the
prompter, arranging his papers by the light of
a long-wick'd flaring candle, with the call-boy
at his elbow, ready to take his orders to the
scene-room, green-room, "flies," or orchestra.
A triumphal march is being performed on one
fiddle, by the musician, whose business it is,
as *repetiteur*, to represent the entire orchestra;
and the Ballet-master is preparing to drill the

female warriors in their grand evolutions. The Coryphées now arrive, as well as the Corps de Ballet ; the former holding a higher rank and receiving a higher salary than the latter. They are pretty trim-built girls, with sallow faces and large eyes—the pallor that overspreads their features resulting from cosmetics and late hours. They work very hard, and get very little sleep ; but they appear to be very merry amongst themselves for all that. They are *petite* in figure, and neatly dress'd in dark stuff cloaks, or check "polkas," and little black velvet or drawn bonnets. The Corps de Ballet immediately prepare to march ; and the others, who will not be wanted until the divertissement in the second act, run up stairs to the wardrobe to see about their dresses.

"Now, ladies ! ladies !" cries the Ballet-master, knocking a tambourine, "we are behind time. Places ! places !"

And the army gets into order, each taking

her gun or other weapon from a bundle leaning against the side of the proscenium, and shouldering it, in her bonnet and shawl.

"Miss Saunders, where's your gun?" asks the Ballet-master, whose eagle eye detects an unarmed Amazon.

"Please, sir, it's not finished yet," is the reply.

"Very well; take this wand."

And the Ballet-master gives her a magician's rod with a serpent twisted round it—a canvas eel stuffed with sawdust and painted—and a Chinese march begins, on one fiddle, thus:—

The Ballet-master is now all excitement. Every time he bangs the tambourine, it is a signal for them to turn, or divide, simultaneously; and they wait for the same signal at night. At last Miss Saunders gets out of step.

"Stop! *stop!!* STOP!!!" roars the master. But orchestral accompaniments and Ballet-girls are as bad to pull up, when once off, as cabs without check-strings. At last, by stamping and thumping the ground with his stick, he succeeds.

"Now, if you please: once more, Mr. Barnard."

And Mr. Barnard begins again.

"Now, then!" shouts the master; "what are you gaping there for? Why don't you move? *Why—the—devil—don't—you—move!!*" [More thumps on the stage.] "Once more, Mr Barnard."

At length Miss Saunders, in extreme terror, by dint of careful counting, begins to know something about it; and then Mr. Barnard is enabled to go off comfortably, as follows:—

An hour has been taken up in this way: and then the full band arrives and "all the ladies and gents." A piece of machinery, like a large gas rake, is lighted up above the orchestra: and the Corps de Bailet and "extras" are dismissed into the pit, to be out of the way, where they begin to cover old satin shoes, and look at the proceedings until wanted again.

And now the rehearsal commences. The flats are taken to their respective grooves and "cuts"—which are those large wooden hinges you see flap down from the top of the wings before a scene changes ; the author—an ingenious person who has a trifling interest in the piece, and ranks, somewhere or another, amongst the supernumeraries and other clever people employed in his production—comes down to the lamps to see what is going on ; and most wonderful creations are let down from the "borders," or top pieces, and hauled up from the unknown depths below the mezzonine floor, which the most indigestible supper only could give birth to, in the region of dreams. In fact it is reported that the celebrated Mr. Fitzball, who lives in a Wolf's Glen, near the Murderer's Road-side Cross, somewhere in Bohemia, and drinks a pint of blood from a skull, fasting every morning, and burns only blue fire in his grate, owes his most thrilling inspirations to a full evening meal of pork chops, Welsh rabbits, turnip-radishes, and cocoa-nuts. But this by the way.

The mezzonine floor, to which we have just
alluded—or "mazarine," as it is called in the
theatre—is the true region of Ballet-girl en-
chantment. It is underneath the theatre—

situated half way between the stage and no-
where—and inhabited solely by those active
spirits of the establishment who send fairies and
demons up and down the traps. It is that
mysterious region which theatrically-inclined
young gentlemen look longingly at, from the
front rows of the pit, when the orchestra goes in
and out through the small door. It is the
abode of good and evil genii. It is the abyss
to which the doomed palace sinks, and from
which the fairy world arises : and grouped here
and there amongst its supports, do the supernumerary devils of the opening scene turn to
the elegant and noble guests of the banquet.

The rehearsal proceeds—arguing, forgetting, stopping, and repeating being its principal
features : and at last the period arrives for the
divertissement, and the Coryphées take their
places on the stage.

It is curious to see them rehearsing their
grand pas in their walking dresses. They di-

vest themselves of their bonnets and shawls;
and sometimes tie a handkerchief, gipsy fashion,
over their heads.   Then they begin—sinking
down and crossing their hands on their breast;

bending back almost to vertebral dislocation;
wreathing their arms; and the like.   You

think if ballets took place, the scenes of which are laid in every-day life, what preposterously absurd things they would be. You will observe, too, that they have all kept their gloves on: it appears to be a point of etiquette amongst them to do so. And they catch the notion of any particular step, or figure, with singular facility: especially those to whom the honour of a place in the front rank is assigned. Sometimes, but very seldom, the stereotypical smile of the evening breaks out at rehearsal, beaming at the dark void of the house before them, or even at the stage manager, who is the nearest approach to the Ogres of old that they can fancy. Otherwise they preserve the greatest gravity—at least those in front: the hinder ones always appear anxious to earn their money, or attract attention both at rehearsal and in the evening. Indeed in the latter case, it is most amusing to watch them—their attitudes and attempts to fascinate are exceedingly diverting, even in the extreme rear, and evidently under the impression that they alone are attracting the attention of the house.

About half past three, or four o'clock, the rehearsal concludes; and the Ballet-girl, very tired, quits the theatre, to be there again a little after six. All this time she has had no refreshment: and she possibly lives over half-an-hour's walk from the theatre. It may be wet, too, and her thin shoes are not very well calculated to meet the treacherous paths and crossings of the suburbs. For in common with most members of the theatrical profession, she lives far from the scene of her labours. We know that an actor generally contrives to pitch his tent at the most inconvenient distance from the theatre that he can possibly accomplish: and hence his whole life is embittered by anxieties to catch midnight 'busses that convey Hammersmithonians to their mild domiciles; or to find friends inclined to go halves in a cab to the outskirts of Brompton.

It is true that with the Ballet-girl this may be for economy : as lodgings are cheaper in the unknown regions of Lambeth, than they would be in the immediate neighbourhood of the theatre. But still this induces other expenses, very trifling though they be. To fifteen shillings a week, however, the smallest sums that it would be dangerous to buy a Bottle Imp with, are of importance. Hence, in her purse, you will always find a small store of half-pence, which she will tell you are "for the bridge." For, as you shall not go over London bridge, at any time, without meeting a white horse; so you shall not cross that of Waterloo, between half past five and seven, or later, after midnight, without meeting an actor or a Ballet-girl.

CHAPTER IV.

OF THE EVENING PERFORMANCE.

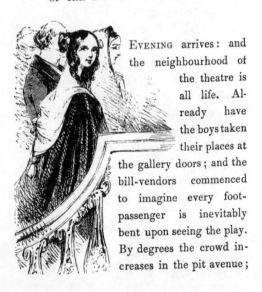

Evening arrives: and the neighbourhood of the theatre is all life. Already have the boys taken their places at the gallery doors; and the bill-vendors commenced to imagine every foot-passenger is inevitably bent upon seeing the play. By degrees the crowd increases in the pit avenue;

and the "orders" collect round the box entrance, resolved, as they are "not admitted after seven o'clock," to be in time. The orange stalls display their best fruit in front of the house: and soon the boiled trotters will be seen at the door of the nearest wine vaults, and the ham sandwich merchant close to the gallery: and the first cab will draw up at the portico, with the man ready to open the door, who has been running in the mud with a bill to the window for the last quarter of a mile, and quarrels with the accredited linkman in consequence. "Mind the step, my lady," says the latter, to establish his position. Just then all the doors open simultaneously, by some mysterious means we never could account for—the pit policeman cries out "Take care of your pockets:" and the gentleman who has three ladies to take care of vainly asks the crowd behind him "What's the use of pushing so?" as he intimates that there will be plenty of room for everybody, about which the crowd appears to entertain a different opinion: whilst at the box entrance, the free list is quite blocked up with orders, in the proportion of ten, to one who pays. Within, the first in the pit rush to the middle of the front rows—box-doors and seats slam and jar—gallery friends keep a place for "Jim!" whom they address by name, or shout for "music!" at least twenty minutes before there is a chance of hearing any—box-keepers look at imaginary lists, on slips of paper, to see if there is any room for you (or rather, if you put your finger and thumb into your waistcoat pocket), and the evening life of the theatre commences.

But before this the Ballet-girl has entered the house by the stage-door; and, with a nod to the hall-keeper to show him that she is there if a bouquet has been sent, and a glance at the rack for a letter, she goes to her room.

Five other sylphs attire with her; and the

room has two long dressers against its sides,
divided into compartments, each containing a
common looking-glass and a few mysterious po-
matum and rouge-pots, combs, powder-dabbers,
scraps of silver-leaves and "logies," and a wash-
hand stand in the middle. And then the toilet
commences, and the dresser has a hard time of
it. For the waist of the dress is too short, or

the skirts too long, or the white comes below
the tarlatan, or the wings won't fit well at all
to the shoulders, but droop down as if they

were going to fall off like those of the Mountain
Sylph.   And such phrases as "Fasten the top
hook and eye, Kate;" or, "Pin my scarf, Loo,
there's a dear;" or, "Am I all right behind?
do tell me, Laura!" with similar ones, are
rapidly and unceasingly uttered, until the call-
boy walks down the corridor, shouting "Over-
ture's begun, ladies!"

A minute or two after they are all in their
places.   The fairies who have got to fly, attach
themselves to the hooks of the "travellers" at
the top of the theatre; those who have to come
up traps go down cellar-stairs to the mezzonine
floor, and get ready upon the winding-up plat-
forms; and the Cracovienne visitors who have
not to appear until the ball in Act 2, go to
their green-room, where there may be a cheval
glass for them to admire themselves in; or, if
not, they steal into the other when nobody is
looking.

All goes on well until the curtain falls upon

Act 1. The march of the Amazons brings down thunders of applause, and radiant are the smiles of the first rank as they come twenty-

four abreast up to the lamps. Be sure there is not one who does not think that if the piece succeeds, it will be owing to her alone. Then the *tableau* is formed; the Act-drop comes down; and in another minute the stage is all confusion.

And now it is an awkward time for the strangers who are behind the scenes. They cannot get anywhere to be out of the way, unless they go into the green-room, which requires much nerve. The carpenters (or scene-shifters, as they are called by the exoteric world) come hastening along with the wings and flats wanted for the second act. The scene-painter is flying here and there, giving his directions for the lighting and placing of the " set;" the stage manager is doing the same, with the addition of a little swearing; the property man is arranging the banquet of *papier mache* apples and empty goblets, or *vin ordinaire* bottles covered with Dutch metal; and the Amazons who have to be visitors in the next scene, run over everybody in their hurry to get to their dressing-rooms.

The loungers of the *coulisses* soon begin

their flirtations with the Coryphées. If you listen you will be astonished to find how feeble is the dialogue in most cases. But it appears to make them—the loungers—perfectly happy, "slow" as it is. Elsewise they would not be there, night after night, with such unvarying regularity.

"Clear!" shouts the prompter—which means that everybody must get off the stage—and the curtain again rises. In this act the Ballet-girl has not so much dancing: she has rather to express the most vivid interest in, and sympathy with, the fortunes, sorrows, or joys of the principal performers. Possibly, no other class of humanity is actuated by so many different sentiments in five minutes. Were the "heart-strings," which poets write of, really bits of cord to pull the feelings into different positions, as the string makes the puppet kick its legs and arms, then you would see that those belonging to a whole Corps de Ballet are tugged at once. For a large party of young ladies, there is singular harmony amongst them. They all feel with equal acuteness the wrongs of the heroine they dance attendance to ; and, at the same moment, they all are simultaneous in their allegiance, when they offer her valuable baskets of flowers, apparently only for inspection, as they always pirouette round, and take them away again immediately. And the shock experienced at the brutality of the rich rival, affects them all as rapidly as the one from the electrifying machine at the Polytechnic Institution, when the misguided visitors on the bottom row in the theatre are beguiled by the persuasive eloquence of the gentleman who lectures, into forming a chain with their hands.

CHAPTER V

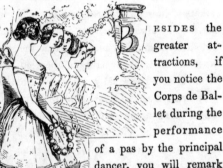

BESIDES the greater attractions, if you notice the Corps de Ballet during the performance of a pas by the principal dancer, you will remark the attention with which they regard it, albeit they have already seen it several scores of times. But they all entertain the

hope of one day being in the same position;
they partake of all her feelings, and they would
applaud as well as the audience if they were

not on the stage, when the favourite crouches forward to the lamps at last, to acknowledge the showers of bouquets and wreaths with which she is greeted. There is not one of the Coryphées whose pulses do not beat quicker at the ovation, as though it belonged to herself.

At length the play is over, and life and noise are active in the thoroughfares adjoining the theatre. The clattering of impatient horses' hoofs, the oaths of the drivers, the commands of policemen, and the hoarse shouts of "Fust keb!" or, "Ham sandwich, pennee!" echo in every direction. From the box-staircase descend crowds of mixed company. First come the "orders" of the upper tier, who always get out first, in bonnets of marvellous fashion, and odd unestablished head-dresses, generally of remarkable originality; for chiefly amongst the female branches of the family tree that blooms upon the stage do the orders appear to be distributed. Then come the Gents—our own Gents—anxiously looking out for some available gas-jet at which to light their cheap cigar and pollute the lobby with its vapour, and believing that unless they did this they would not be considered "swellish" either by their brotherhood of acquaintances, or the crowd of utter strangers around them. Many do this and walk off. Many others wait within the doors to stare at the dress-circle company as they descend, and imbibe the odours of Patchouli and Bouquet de la Reine that float about the rustling forms of the handsome women who, clustered together in sheltered corners of the entrance, await the arrival of their carriages— their cool polished shoulders wrapped by heavy shawls, and their perfumed tresses imprisoned by coquettish little hoods of artful worsted work. And many from the pit come to this station to get the credit of having been to the boxes all this time, as is still the

case with Gents at the Adelphi, where the
transit from one egress to the other is easily
made.

The play is over, and the supper-rooms in
the neighbourhood fill proportionately. Waiters
tumble over one another in their frantic hurry,
and take devilled kidneys to the guest who has
ordered nothing but a go of gin; or insist upon
serving a Welsh rabbit and a mighty goblet of
the ponderous entire to the contented gentleman
who, in a state of excellent repletion, is enjoying his cigar and building all sorts of agreeable castles on its wreathed smoke, ere it is lost
in the haze that hangs about the room. And
the oyster-man at the Albion! believe us, he has
a sad time of it, as he Vandykes about the room
from box to box with his tripod tub, vainly
endeavouring to open the tight bivalves as fast
as his customers can eat them; and, miscalcu-
lating the quantities devoured, in his confusion,
by pitching the shells into the wrong division.

For it requires great coolness and decision of character to open oysters properly. It is an art learned only by long practice; like throwing at snuff-boxes, playing at the pea and thimble, cutting up ducks, and doing the reverse step in the *Deux Temps*, and may not be wildly undertaken. And herein do those who send barrels of natives to their friends, cause as much domestic misery as though they had flung grenades, instead of shells, into the bosoms of families. Every one becomes a Tantalus; the treat is in his grasp, but he cannot touch it. And after pinning his hand to the mahogany table with a knife at least half-a-dozen times, he produces a wretched mass of some anomalous substance, torn in half as it clings to each shell, and tasting something between a periwinkle and a gravel walk.

But all this by the way; for it has little to do with the actions of the Ballet-girl at this particular time. She resumes her walking-

dress, and, stealing out at the stage door,
passes unnoticed through the small crowd that
clusters about it to watch the egress of the ar-

tistes; and trips away to her home (over the
water), scarcely glancing to the right or left,

but hurrying on with her shawl drawn closely round her.

And when she gets home,—which is, in all probability, a residence very different to the fairy bowers she lately inhabited—she finds a very humble supper left out for her; or perhaps none at all, not counting the bottle of ginger-beer she had at the late shop where the pies are always steaming so furiously in the open window.

And then she goes to bed, only worried with the thoughts of the call to-morrow morning—to " cut " the new piece where it hung fire, and alter some of its dances. With the music, the stage, and the lights still haunting her senses she falls asleep; and perhaps dreams that she is a second Taglioni, and that foreign gentlemen, the likes of which have never been seen even in Leicester Square, are dragging her from the Theatre to the hotel, in her own carriage.

And thus finishes a day of the Ballet-girl's business life.

CHAPTER VI.

OF THE BALLET-GIRL AT SOIREES DANSANTES.

PUTTING the theatre out of the question, the Ballet-girl is passionately fond of dancing. One would think she had enough of it in her profession; but it is not so: the greatest treat she knows is to go to a public ball and wear a *costume de société*.

And here, though she does not leave the
theatre until midnight, she will keep on dancing with untiring vigour until seven in the
morning; she would even have the concluding
Post Horn Galop encored, if the musicians
had strength left to perform it. And she never
betrays her profession in her dancing: all is
orderly, quiet, in great propriety. At the time
when everybody was learning the Polka, several
of the teachers of dancing selected three or four
Coryphées from the theatres for the pupils to
practice with; and in this manner they ac-
quired a perfect knowledge of the deportment
observed in average society. They learnt this
readily, for they are naturally quick and
perceptive. But they also know the best ball-
room conduct of the highest classes: how they
pick this up we will now see.

The two favourite resorts of the Ballet-girl
are, the Portland Rooms and Weippert's: they
may be met with at the Hanover-square Rooms

and Willis's, at many of the advertising half-guinea balls for charities; but the two former are their favourite resorts. As Weippert's, however, has simply the characteristics of a very well conducted public ball, we will confine ourselves to the latter resort of the dance-loving "*jeunes gens.*"

It does not imply reprehensible ignorance on the part of anybody not to know the Portland Rooms: but, as an odd phase in the mighty kaleidoscope of London life—a comical intermingling of the various heterogeneous components which, shaken together, form such strange figures—the place is worth a visit. Whereabouts it is we cannot exactly say. We only know that it is between the Middlesex Hospital and the extinguisher-spired church in Langham place—the apex of which would be such an uncomfortable point to alight upon if you were to fall out of a balloon directly over it. And this latter landmark would never have been dis-

covered, at least as we imagine, but for a festive
gentleman, who early one morning, slightly
overcome with the champagne of the Maryle-
bone vintage (a celebrated wine to which we
owe the origin of the phrase "playing up old
gooseberry"), and not having money withal to
pay his cab, suddenly, to his utter bewilder-
ment, emerged into Regent Street. But he
never found the way back again; like the cap-
tain of the Forty Thieves, he returned often,
but to no avail. He only recollected, from his
mental haziness on the night in question, that
the street had two corners at its end; and when
he came back again, he found that in this respect all the thoroughfares were alike. And so
at last he gave it up despairingly, and went his
way. Once, it is said, a caravan of students
started from the Middlesex to lay down the
journey accurately; but, the anatomical de-
monstrator having banished half-and-half from
the dissecting-room, the open doors of the

Spread Eagle hostelry, and the civility of Mistress Sealey the hostess, proved too great a temptation to be passed by. And thus did those young gentlemen, of ill-regulated minds, spend the day in luxury and harmonic indolence; and the geography of the country round still remains a mystery.

But the Portland Rooms evidently exist; for if, on certain days, you look in the morning papers, and on others, in the *Sunday Times*, you will see an announcement similar to this:—

PORTLAND ROOMS, Foley-street, Portland-place.—Mr. HENRY has the honour to announce that his next SOIREE DANSANTE will take place on Wednesday next, and, in consequence of the success attending them this season, they will take place every alternate Wednesday. Dancing to commence at 10 o'clock. Tickets 2s. 6d. each. Mr. and Mrs. Henry give lessons in all the fashionable dances at all hours, either at this academy or the residence of pupils.

Mr. Henry is in the ballet at the Opera, and he married Mrs. Henry, formerly Miss Dott, from the Corps de Ballet; she is a quiet pretty little person with dark eyes and hair, and mother of one or two small Henrys, on the high-road to preferment as flying fairies. Mrs. Henry has sisters, also in the ballet, who will be at the ball; and have dances of their own every month or so.

Arriving at the Portland Rooms, somehow or another—a Hansom is safest—you will find the door lighted up, with a few hack carriages loitering about, as well as one or two private Broughams; and one dashing cab, or so, with the servant inside asleep, and the horse looking as though he was listening to an amateur five-act play. If you please, you leave your *Gibus* with the attendant; if not, you can take it into the room unchallenged, and without having to combat the door-keeper for the right of so doing, as is the case at balls at the London Tavern, where they don't understand such strange conduct. And then you receive a programme printed on a little card, as follows :—

Mr. Henry's Ball.

LA DANSE.

1. QUADRILLE Pastorale . . . Mysteries of Paris.
2. LANCERS . . . . Original.
3. SPANISH DANCE.
4. QUADRILLE (Trenise) . . Enchantress.
5. POLKA . . . . German.
6. CALEDONIANS.
7. CELLARIUS WALTZ.
8. QUADRILLE Pastorale . . Esmeralda.
9. REDOWA WALTZ.
10. POLKA . . . . Bridal.

11. SIR ROGER DE COVERLY,
12. QUADRILLE (Trenise) . . Don Pasquale.
13. POLKA . . . . The Elfin.
14. WALTZ.
15. QUADRILLE Pastorale . . Maritana.
16. POLKA . . . . Bohemian.
17. QUADRILLE (Trenise) . . Alma.
18. CIRCULAR WALTZ and POST HORN GALOP.
19. QUADRILLE Pastorale . . Irish.
20. POLKA . . . . Cricket.
21. QUADRILLE Pastorale . . Royal Irish.

Mr. Henry returns thanks for the honor.

Mrs. Henry's Dress Ball is fixed for the 21st Instant.

Miss Dott gives Lessons in all the fashionable Dances.

The room is long and narrow, with a row of seats down each side; and at the end, over the

fireplace, is the music gallery, in which, as far
as work goes, some performers are certainly
earning their money. A polka is going on, and
if you know a few of the leading West-end men
by sight, you will be somewhat surprised at
meeting them.

For so it is. Amidst the confused throng
of polkers—turning, chasing, and banging
against each other in all directions—are many
accustomed to flutter hearts in circles far different to the one in which they are now dancing
with such indefatigable good temper. And
many fair girls, whose veins swell with the
gentlest blood in England, and whose names are
in the most patrician divisions of the Blue Book,
would give all their world for the tithe of the
attention which the cavaliers are bestowing upon
the pretty Coryphées who are now their partners. Whether it is that in escaping from the
restrictions of the cold etiquette which they are
called upon habitually to preserve, they give

their pent-up spirits full play; or whether the
very pleasure derived from plunging into the
extreme of life's antitheses, is the incentive, we
know not.   But here they are, "taking the
shine out" of the ruck of dancers in first-rate
style, and completely winding up all the aspiring
Gents who try to outdo them.   For thorough-
bred blood and build is as much inherent in
men as in horses.

The ceremonies of introduction at the Portland Rooms are not *de rigueur*: indeed they
may almost be considered Arcadian, from their
simplicity.   A quadrille is formed, and the
master of the ceremonies cries out, "Side cou-
ple wanted!" which always appears to be the
case; and which he utters perpetually, wildly
and mechanically, even before any one stands
up.   And then you will see the Ballet-girl
take her place with her partner, in a dress of
faultless make and cerise tarlatan, perfectly
quiet and ladylike in her demeanour, and very

F

different, in repose, to her *vis-a-vis*, who is the daughter of a baker, with a wreath in her head that looks as if it was made of green leaves and mixed biscuit, and a brooch in her bosom as big as a penny open jam tart, and something like one.

You will be struck with the nice method of her dancing. She does not bow to her partner and then to the corners, as many of the company do: but her face beams with excitement as the *Esmeralda* quadrilles begin :—

for then she thinks of Carlotta, and her tambourine, and the joyous dance of the Truands, in the *Cour des Miracles*, and all the stirring points of the most charming ballet ever composed.

And now the *Truandaise*, she knows, will come
in the *L'Eté* :—

and when that pretty air commences, it is only
by great strength of mind that she can refrain
from dancing the tripping *pas* appropriate to it;

but one of the "Pets of the Guards" is her *vis-
a-vis* and she maintains her usual deportment.
So the quadrille goes on to its conclusion ; and
then she thinks she should like some lemonade,
upon which, she descends to the refreshment
room—a locality we shall presently describe—
with her partner ; and indulges in the efferves-
cing beverages, until a sound is heard, something like this : —

when nothing in the world would keep her
down stairs longer, and she hurries up to the
ball-room. Her partner has been as eagerly
looking after her, and they are soon in the
thickest of the Polka *mêlée*.

And now it is that the Ballet-girl with her cavalier distinguish themselves from the Snobs. For the latter social nuisances fling their legs about; and get in everybody's way; and turn their heads to the right and left shoulder alternately, as they twist about; and plunge; and dive; and commit every species of maniacal enormity: whilst you will see our graceful cou-

ple avoiding everybody—their heads over each
other's right shoulders—their arms extended,
and adroitly dropped when they anticipate a
collision, moving easily about in all directions
without one concussion. And when this is
over, supper time arrives.

The supper-room at the Portland-rooms is
a very curious place indeed ; something like
the cabin of a steam-boat with a window at the
upper end, level with the floor of the ball-room,
through which you see nothing but ankles.
There are long tables down the room covered
with tea-things ; and three huge coffee-pots on
the fire as big as drums, and plates of ham, and
pats of butter, and cottage loaves. The presence of shrimps alone is wanted to make you
believe at once that you are going to Gravesend,
with the exception that the coffee, or beer,
or whatever is poured out, keeps quite still, instead of jogging and vibrating, into centrifugal
circles, as it does on board the steamers.

The room is pretty full. Cups and saucers are clattering, lemonade corks are popping out of their prisons, knives are clinking on plates, and voices are in full cry everywhere. The Ballet-girl, you will find, prefers stout to champagne—she says that wine makes her giddy; and she has a great notion of coffee, even for supper. And then there are such jokes—such famous, unapproachable jokes—bandied about (especially at the little round table in the corner of the room, where the best style of men and the prettiest girls are assembled), that none were ever heard like them; and such laughter, and such great fun altogether, that you can think of nothing else but a supper-scene from the old French memoirs.

At last, when they have all eaten enough—which is not in a minute, for the Ballet-girl requires sustenance—they think of joining the ball again. "Polk*ar!*" shouts Mr. Henry. "Take your partners for the Polk*ar!*"

And in another moment they are hard at work dancing it.

An after-supper Polka at the Portland Rooms is a thing to see. It generally commences with the pupils of the professional gentleman who gives the ball, many of whom have their hairs curled, and wear pumps and frock coats, and at times lay-down collars and Byron ties. These start off at first under great difficulties, as nobody will get out of the way and let them do their steps, which is a great point with them; for they go the entire Polka. And when they have knocked, and trodden, and kicked the idlers out of the way, then the *élite* come in with their stylish little partners, and take the shine out of all the others in marvellous style; making little steps, and acting on the very "confidential" manner of dancing with their arms out, and the fair little heads of their partners almost reclining against the coral studs of their elaborate cambric breastplates—in lieu

of the steel they sometimes carry, and in which
you may see not a few of them cased up in the
corridor on Drawing-room days. They keep
the centre of the room, where they are less
likely to be upset, and turn and reverse in a
manner "pleasant to behold," as Old Pepys
would say, had he lived now to write his diary.
Nor are they less graceful in *Trenise* or

Pastorale. The Ballet-girl prefers *Pastorale*, creeping up to their *vis-a-vis* with little steps, and a position of similar confidence and sympathy.

And by all this, and the crowd coming in after, there is kicked up such a mighty dust that one might almost imagine the rooms were never swept, by a connivance between the proprietor and the man who sells the lemonade down stairs, at sixpence a bottle, to wash out the throats of the Polkers.

There is a temporary lull; and then the first notes of the charming Bridal Waltz sound something like

and they are all off again. And this continues until the programme is exhausted; and the cabs that have been so long waiting take the

Ballet-girls to their homes, which are chiefly second floors, occasionally first, and have all got street doors with large key-holes, and pluralities of bell-pulls at their posts.

And then the Portland-rooms are deserted, except by the pupils of Miss Dott, anxious to acquire the fashionable dances, until the following Wednesday week, when the scene is enacted all over again.

CHAPTER VII.

OF GREENWICH AND BLACKWALL.

B RIGHT are the days now (June beginning to be kept as festivals at the river-side; and unequalled are the dinners at the Trafalgar and Brunswick.

It is pleasant to see the blue river as you dine, sparkling in the sun-light, and flowing on with its freight of ships; to watch the short steamers, swarming with life, cutting the water in their rapid course, or the heavy continental boats slowly making their way towards the turbulent waters of the channel; to criticize the trim yachts brought up, almost to the very windows; or trace the dusky colliers following one another from the Pool, in grave and dirty procession, tacking, and drifting, and then making the various turns of the river until they appear in the distance to be sailing in the very fields and waste lands.

And on land there is an equal quantity of life to amuse you, as the dashing four-in-hands are driven up to the door, and Mr. Hart (and perhaps his tiny dog) comes out to receive the men who people them. But the carriages are not all four-in-hands. There are indolent easy devil-may-care private cabs; and sly wicked Broughams; and mail phaetons trying to look boyish and in the mode, driven by men who do the same; and perhaps a rackety stock-exchange dog-cart, or a heavy old chariot, or a feeble-minded fly. And altogether they make a goodly array, and lead thinking minds to wonder where all the white-bait is to come from that is to appease the appetites of their inmates.

And no one wonders at it more than the Ballet-girl, who likes white-bait, but does not altogether believe that they are fish. She does not, however, profess any very great predilection for them: on the contrary, she thinks shrimps and 'winkles the finer productions of nature. But the journey to Greenwich, by the steamer, is very pleasant; and the air is purer, and the sun brighter at Greenwich and Blackwall than in Drury-lane or the Strand; and cider-cup is such a wonderful beverage; and brown bread and butter such marvellous eating; and above all, a table near the window—she does not object to the coffee-room—overlooking

the river, is "so very nice," that the white-bait, being the excuse for enjoying these things, gains with her a greater importance than it would otherwise do. And we say—in fear and trembling, though, of being cried down—that perhaps there are many with whom it does the same. We could not eat white-bait, away from the river, for any money. We have heard that Berthollini provides it : no doubt if he does, it is very fine ; but we believe it to be a fiction, and to be considered in his bill of fare in company with those mystic untried dishes, Polpette, Sambaion, and Cramouski à la Russe.

Passing over whether she believes in whitebait or not, a dinner at Greenwich is with the Ballet-girl an extraordinary treat. She is not particular as to the rank or position of her companion, so that he is a gentleman ; but she prefers one who is "great fun." She will not think him coarse if he can show her a conjuring trick with the almonds and raisins, cut a swan out of an apple, make an orange basket ; or do clever feats with bits of biscuit.

But she has a great notion of an author, not on account of his intellectual standard, but because she sees that he does not stand in awe of the stage-manager. She meets him too at rehearsals, and other theatrical gatherings, in which all appear to have a mutual interest : and looks upon him as a sort of link between her profession and the world outside the theatre walls. And when the authors make a little money, which is a rare occurrence, by selling books of their plays in a theatre ; and are single and free, they are just as happy to dine at Greenwich as their pretty companions. And then they promise that in the next drama there shall be a few lines for her to speak. But promises made over cider-cup and floating pieces of Wenham lake ice, that bob so coolly against the upper lip, are not always kept.

The journey home is very pleasant; especially if it be by water, and the night is warm and moonlit. For the Ballet-girl has a very nice ear, generally speaking, for music: and if you but lead up to it she will sing all the ballet airs you best remember, as you sit snugly at the stern of the boat, steaming up the pool. She will recall the dying chords of Giselle; the brilliant fête of Alma; the letter-worshipping devotion of Esmeralda; the leafy guard of Eoline; and the musical affection of the Peri: until you will almost expect to see her skim off across the glistening Thames, or perform a *Pas de l'ombre* on the steamboat.

We are afraid to ask the question; but how is it that these airs, and similar ones, bring back such floods of emotions to our bosoms, when High Art, and the compositions it is most proud of, never affect us at all? We shall most probably be told that we have not the mind to enter into them. We suppose not.

CHAPTER VIII.

OF THE BALLET-GIRL CONSIDERED AS OF
THE INDUSTRIOUS CLASSES.

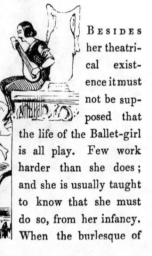

B E S I D E S
her theatri-
cal exist-
ence it must
not be sup-
posed that
the life of the Ballet-girl
is all play. Few work
harder than she does;
and she is usually taught
to know that she must
do so, from her infancy.
When the burlesque of

Cinderella was running at the Lyceum theatre,
there was a dance of little children in it—mites
of five and seven years old and upwards, who
performed in the manner of the Danseuses
Viennoises. They were not wanted until the
last scene, and one of these children made no
inconsiderable addition to her few shillings
weekly salary by knitting worsted head-dresses
for ladies, whilst she was unemployed in the
green-room. For it behoves the Ballet-girl
to be a good workwoman. Shoes have to be
covered and gloves to be mended; for shoes
and gloves are expensive affairs at any time,
and particularly so when obliged to be bought
out of fifteen shillings a week. Consequently,
it is by no means an uncommon thing to see
the fairy lay down all her supernatural attributes and wreathed smiles upon quitting the
stage, and take up, in their place, a piece of
work that she has to finish. And then she
will begin to ply the needle very industriously,

the whiles she sits comfortably by the side of
the evil demon of the piece, to whom she is
opposed; and both together enter into a little
domestic or general conversation with the

libertine lord, whom the aforesaid evil spirit is eventually to take down the trap.

The Ballet-girl is not always, however, engaged in simple sewing. We have at times noticed her passing horse-hair through tiny beads, or making a small labyrinthine sack of netted silk, which she was pleased to call a purse, for her especial favourite; for she has generally an *amant*—a sweetheart—an intended if you will. Understand us, we are not treading on any equivocal ground; it is a fair and honest attachment, and one not often affected by all the plaudits of the audience, or the butterfly attentions of the *coulisses*. He may be connected with the theatre, he may be altogether in another line of life; but he is usually found waiting at the stage-door to escort her home, and he forms a portion of the crowd assembled there at the conclusion of the performance—real amateurs, for the most part, in theatrical matters, who wait to see the leading

actors in their ordinary dresses, walking like
ordinary persons; or the *prima donna* stepping
into her Brougham; and then go home, more
delighted at the sight than at anything they
have seen on the stage.

The Ballet-girl is a " blanchisseuse" as well
as a " couturière." She has in general, at home,

a little iron, which she regards as the head of
her household gods, for by its aid she is enabled to appear at the balls, in what she considers to be a becoming manner; and herein she
again assimilates to the grisette. If you were
to take her by surprise on the morning of a ball,
you would find her lodgings converted into a
perfect miniature laundry, and you would possibly see her " getting up" the dress in which,
at night, she intends to be the belle of belles.
And the chances are she has made it herself;
or else she is on terms of even visiting fami-
liarity with some wonderfully cheap milliner,
who is sometimes paid in coin of the realm
altogether, or sometimes gets a little money
and a card that passes two into the upper
boxes, whither she goes with her own " young
man" and assumes a pretty gentility with the
position, even refusing to eat an orange if in
the front seat. But the front seats of the
upper tiers are usually let—that is to say, to
all inquiries as to their state by the orders.

The Ballet-girl has more frequently a mother than a father: a singular provision of nature appears to have denied the latter parent to them. We knew one once. He worked for an upholsterer, and lived in Gray's Inn Lane; but he did not give one at all the idea of a being who brought up fairies and mountain sylphs about his hearth. He was usually overcome with beer, and he smoked a pipe of curtailed dimensions. But, such as he was, he was the only one of his kind we ever came into contact with, and the impression was not favourable, founded on that single specimen.

But they have all got mothers, who are the ladies-patronesses of strange bonnets and abnormal dresses. The more rigid ones come to the theatre every night to fetch their daughters home, and are allowed by the stage-doorkeeper to stand inside his lodge, and near the fire in winter. And in no manner will they permit any one else to see their young ladies home, unless he pays them very great attention, or is their proper accepted admirer. And even then he must, to find great favour in the eyes of the mother, be somehow or another connected with the profession.

And indeed the object of the Coryphée in marriage is not altogether to be taken out of the theatre—generally the reverse. A very large proportion of the young persons now enumerated in the Corps de Ballet of the various houses as "Miss" Such-a-one, are married. And, married or single, we speak advisedly in saying that nothing can be more exemplary than the conduct of the ballet generally, taken as a mass. Many of them—in several instances two or three sisters—contribute, in a great degree, to the support of their family, either by their salaries (which may be averaged at a guinea a-week in the more respectable theatres), or by teaching dancing on their own account. An intimate acquaintance with the internal economy of a theatre, and the fortunes of those assisting to form its company, enables us to state earnestly that amongst no other class have we witnessed more domestic devotion, or readiness at all times to proffer mutual assistance, in the event of accident or other misfortune, than in the Corps de Ballet; and that, in contradiction to the notions of the Gents, by no others have we seen any transgression against propriety, or advances even supposed to be questionable, more effectually repulsed. We do not deny that there are several who cannot lay claim to a reputation entirely unblemished; but it is as false as it is uncharitable to suppose that the attributes of those few are alike characteristic of the entire class.

CHAPTER IX.

OF VARIOUS IDIOSYNCRASIES.

 **THE** BALLET-GIRL is, we believe, the nearest approach to the Parisian grisette—the grisette '*pur sang*' of the *Quartier Latin*—that we have in England. Our ordinary classes of young females engaged in various manufactures, from milliners to book-stitchers, shoe-binders, and the like, have little

in common with their continental sisters. But putting her connection with the theatre on one side, the Ballet-girl has many points in common with the little *brodeuses*, *couturières*, and *illumineuses* of the transpontine districts of Paris.

She is small, trim, *une petite taille bien prise*, as Paul de Kock would say, and blessed with a light heart that allows her to laugh merrily upon all occasions : and, as we have seen, she is very fond of a dance. Under any circumstances she likes a dance : in private ; or as a peasant girl who believes greatly in the virtues of the Ballet-bride or as a female demon of fire ; or a dryad ; or a fairy ; or a gipsy ; or even as a young Bohemian hussar, at a grand feast of *papier maché* given by the nobleman whom Mr. Howell personates with so much elegance.

As the grisette has, above all things, a passion for galette and chesnuts—not bursting *marrons*

de lyon—so does the principal weakness of the Ballet-girl lie in oysters and porter.   A dozen of the former, she is not particular that they be small, and a pint of the latter, perhaps amongst

three, carried by hook or by crook into the dressing-room, will form a perfect festival, bolted between the *Pas de Fées* of the opening scene and the villagers' *Mazourka* of the closing one, while the costume is changed.

She believes in realities to eat more than theatrical folks do generally. For these usually put their trust alone in the primary formations of the world in which they move. They look upon things that are simply real as unnatural, because they have never been taught to hold commune with them. Painted curtains are with them more true than actual drapery; pasteboard pies are more like what they are intended to represent than the things themselves: their fish must be made of canvas, stuffed with wool, bran, or sawdust: their images of paste-board. And they would not believe in the representation of any street row, wherever it might be, in which fish and images did not come off badly. But all this by the way.

Apart from the bouquets left for her, at times, at the stage-door by the would-be " fast man" (who sits in the stalls every night to see her wear them, and tell his friends, with a wink, that he sent them and that he is all right there) she is, like the grisette again, remarkably at-tached to flowers. You may see several little *danseuses* lingering about the plants in Covent Garden Market, after rehearsal, on sunny spring afternoons ; and the chances are ten to

one but that at home she has an hyacinth, or
some heath; nay, she will sow French beans
rather than not have anything: and she has a
bird, a smoked canary with an uneven tail,
who never sings.   But this she attributes to

his moulting, and so always makes him take saffron, until it is wonderful that he does not turn to an orange colour.

She is very proud of being permitted to say a few words on the stage. A message, or a small reply to a Peri Queen, she thinks more of than the most effective dance : because then she approaches the condition of an actress. And if she has a choice of costume, you will find, that above all things, she loves to be a *debardeur ;* which at first she confounded with

the wandering minstrel of romance, and called a "*doubadour.*" But now she knows better; albeit the hair-dresser's assistant does not, as may be known by inquiries of the ingenious Mr. Wilson, in the Strand. And if the management permits her to wear a wreath of her own purchasing whilst her sister fays go without one, she has achieved another great position, and dreams of one day equalling Carlotta Grisi. For upon inquiry you will find that Carlotta is the real pet of the Ballet.

CHAPTER X.

THE CONCLUSION.

OTHERWISE her disposition is level enough. Little affected by the circumstances by which she is surrounded, she follows her profession as the merest matter of business, in spite of the spells she assists in working upon the public. And, indeed, however charming may be the transient

combination of gauze, spangles, and pink
tights; flowers, wings, and coloured fire; yet
the ideality of these attractions is more than
knocked over by the mundane oaths of the
stage-manager, or the chilling dreary reality of
a morning rehearsal.

The Ballet-girl is very fond of finery. In
a position where so much depends upon effect,
this passion is, in some degree, excusable; and
for this reason effect is the great end desired.
She believes in the jewellery of the Lowther
Arcade to a great degree: that emporium
stands higher with her than ever did the firm
of Storr and Mortimer, with its warmest and
most wealthy patrons. And herein lies her
greatest danger. The handsome presents made
to some of these girls—who work so very hard
at so very small a salary—might well turn their
heads; as might the offers of a splendid settle-
ment or establishment, contrasted with their, in
most cases, very humble homes.